Mary Kooy

2004

To:

From:

When You Thought I Wasn't Looking

A Book of Thanks for Mom

Mary Rita Schilke Korzan

**Andrews McMeel
Publishing**

Kansas City

For my mother,

Blanche Schilke,

my greatest inspiration.

Acknowledgments

Being all of five foot two since the age of thirteen, I have long believed good things come in small packages. I hope this book is no exception. There are more people to thank for its realization than there are pages that fill this book. Nonetheless, there have been those who believed in *When You Thought I Wasn't Looking* since its inception and I would be remiss not to honor them here. My mom, for understanding the monumental love behind such simple words. My husband, Lee, who kept the car steady and quipped, "You made the cut!" when I discovered my poem in *Chicken Soup*. My sisters, Carol and Karen, for being my angel helpers. My children, Jen, Andrea, and Josh, for not rolling their eyes upon hearing my story for the millionth time and whose hugs I could not live without. To Bill Moor (writer extraordinaire), who took the time to listen to my story and to be my friend. My friends, especially Adrianne, Lynn, Cyndee, and Cindy, who give feet to the word friendship. To my editor, Polly Blair, who is personally responsible for my feet no longer touching the ground.

when you thought
I wasn't looking,

You hung my first painting
on the refrigerator
And I wanted to
paint another.

When you thought
I wasn't looking,

You fed a stray cat
And I thought it was good
to be kind to animals.

When you thought
I wasn't looking,

You baked a birthday cake
just for me
And I knew that little things
were special things.

When you thought
I wasn't looking,

You said a prayer
And I believed there was
a God that I could
always talk to.

When you thought
I wasn't looking,

You kissed me good night
And I felt loved.

when you thought
I wasn't looking,

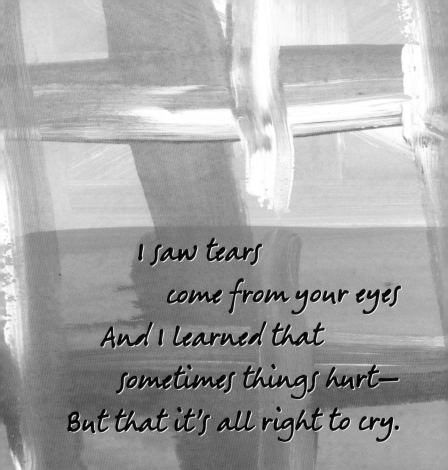

I saw tears
       come from your eyes
And I learned that
       sometimes things hurt—
But that it's all right to cry.

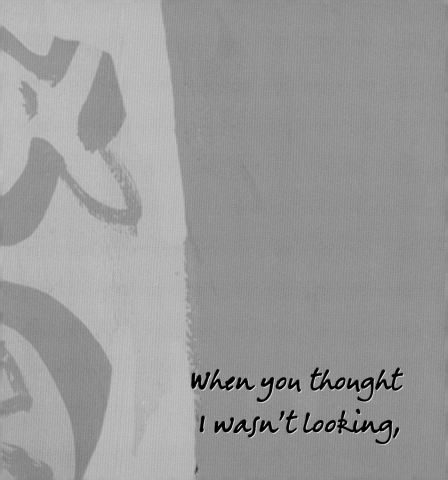

When you thought
I wasn't looking,

You smiled
And it made me want to look
that pretty, too.

When you thought
I wasn't looking,

You cared
And I wanted to be
everything I could be.

When you thought
I wasn't looking—I looked . . .
And wanted to say thanks
For all those things you did
When you thought
I wasn't looking.

The Story Behind
When You Thought I Wasn't Looking

"How do you explain a miracle?" A small group of children recently responded to my question with thoughtful candor. Taylor (age nine) told me, "It's like something that can't really happen, like when someone dies and comes back to life." Andrea (age thirteen) confided, "It's God's love. It's Him telling us how much He loves us."

To me, the story behind *When You Thought I Wasn't Looking* mirrors these insightful definitions. If not a miracle, how else do you explain how a mother's love, translated into a few simple words, traveled from my small hometown in Elyria, Ohio, to hearts all over the world?

Through the years there have been people who have altered my poem, adding to or "improving" its text for their own purposes. Still others have attempted to claim it as their own creative endeavor. For those who wonder about the true origin of this work, it is my esteemed pleasure to share with you the following story.

As I stood on the brink of my adult life, it didn't take much reflection to realize I owed a debt of gratitude to many who helped me along the way. However, it was my mother more than any other who taught me by example and inspired me. I whispered a prayer and asked God to give me the words to thank my mom for all she had done to bring me to that point in my life. The words came. I cannot explain it, but even as my pen was flying across the paper recording the words for *When You Thought I Wasn't Looking,* there was a sense that there was something greater than myself at work. For this reason, I feel I don't have the authority to change its flow, its meaning. I am the steward—the protector of this incredible gift.

My mom read *my poem* for the first time following my college graduation (June 14, 1980) when I presented her with a framed copy, which to this day graces a wall in her living room. Six days after my graduation from Bowling Green State University I was married to Lee Korzan in a magical candlelight ceremony at St. Mary's Church in our hometown of Elyria, Ohio. At the reception that followed, I played my guitar and sang a medley of songs as my way of thanking guests for being an honored part of our day. As a surprise, I decided to conclude my medley with a musical rendition of *When You Thought I Wasn't Looking*. It was an amazing moment. Love enveloped the entire room. Afterward, when guests asked for copies, I knew my tribute had been understood and well received. Not wanting to disappoint anyone to whom I had promised a copy, prints were made and tucked into thank-you notes that went out that summer. I thought that was the end of the story. God apparently had other plans. You see, it was really only the beginning.

Fast-forward seventeen years to June 6, 1997. While we traveled from our home in Indiana to my sister's home in Columbus, Ohio, I read *A Fourth Course of Chicken Soup for the Soul,* which had been a Mother's Day gift from my husband and three children. When I turned to page 136, *When You Thought I Wasn't Looking* glared back at me like some kind of ghost. I screamed while my husband tried to keep his concentration on the wheel. My first thought was that he had done something on the computer and somehow added to the text of the book. Then, as I tried to remind myself to breathe, I noticed two words at the bottom of the page: "Author Unknown."

How did my mother's tribute find its way to the pages of this best-seller? Answers came as we unraveled the mystery one book at a time. The authors of *Chicken Soup* gleaned it from *Stories for the Heart,* compiled by Alice Gray. Ms. Gray first spotted my words in a book titled *Learning to Love When Love Isn't Easy,* written by Dr. David Walls. We learned as we continued our query that Dr. Walls is a minister in my hometown, where I first shared my poem publicly. Dr. Walls explained that he had been given a copy of my poem without my name. Could it have been from someone who attended our wedding?

That remains a mystery. Nonetheless, it struck a chord with him and he included it in his book. Thus it launched the life of my poem in its "Author Unknown" form.

Since that shocking discovery in 1997, *When You Thought I Wasn't Looking* has been put to song by Christian music artist Clint Elias, who hails from Alberta, Canada. It also continues to find a home in countless publications, including these distinguished books: *Love Is Kind*, by Jeff Roberts; *Moor or Less*, by Bill Moor; *Mother O' Mine: A Mother's Treasury*, by Mary Engelbreit; *Staying Up Up Up in a Down Down World*, by Zig Ziglar; and *Stories for the Family's Heart*, *A Pleasant Place*, and *Keepsakes for the Heart*, by Alice Gray.

I've received many calls, letters, and e-mails from kindhearted people all over the world who have taken the time to share with me how my poem has touched their lives. There is obvious truth in the wisdom "That which is given from the heart comes back tenfold." Surprisingly, not all stories are about loving mothers or daughters, as you might expect. Somehow, words of the heart transcend the boundaries of age and gender, as

proven by a letter that arrived in my mailbox one January afternoon. Although I am a stranger to the writer, a young woman, she shared part of her soul in telling me of her incredible experience. Her words stopped me cold and brought me to tears. I will share with you an excerpt of her words, which have forever enriched my life:

> I read your story in *Chicken Soup for the Soul* and a few months after I read it, my father died from emphysema. I am an only child and my mom died a few weeks after I was born. My dad never remarried, so it was just me and him. It was a great loss. I read your story at my father's funeral and it touched my family's heart the same way it touched mine. I will remember your story till it is my turn to go. I wanted to say thank you for giving me the chance to tell my father how I really felt. God bless you and your family.

When You Thought I Wasn't Looking has opened doors to friendships I never even dreamed possible. I do not take these gifts for granted. In fact, I am more and more in awe of how God has chosen to use these words to connect people in a multitude of settings. My mother went about her daily life raising six children, never thinking her actions, such as hanging a painting on the refrigerator or kissing her children good night, would one day influence the world.

A miracle? If not, I choose to think it is no less than God's love. As this poem continues to travel the world via book, Internet, and refrigerator door, I want people to know there is an author to this piece. Even more, I want people to know there is someone very special who inspired it. Generosity isn't her motto. It's her life. Other people talk about love. She personifies it. She is the yardstick by which I measure goodness and integrity. Her friends call her an angel, a living saint, a pillar of faith. I get to call her Mom.

Thanks to all the people who have shared in this blessing and taken the time to make me aware of your stories. I wish you love and . . . blessings.